Don't Be Stupid about Critical Thinking

DontBeStupid.club Reveals 11 Principles for Problem Solving and Good Decision Making

H. Granville James

ITSUS PRESS

Don't Be Stupid about Critical Thinking
DontBeStupid.club Reveals 11 Principles for
Problem Solving and Good Decision Making

Legal Disclaimer: Everything in this book is the opinion of
the author. No responsibility is taken for the application or
use of these thoughts in any specific circumstances. The
reader should *Think for Yourself*.

ISBN: 1530919568
ISBN-13: 978-1530919567

Contents

1.
Let's Begin

STUPID (ADJECTIVE) - SHOWING a lack of thought or good judgment.

Critical thinking is the smart person's weapon against stupidity. Using critical thinking, your decisions make life easier. Stupid people struggle with basic life questions. If they can't find it on Google, they're lost.

Critical thinkers make decisions for themselves. They use many resources to gather information, consider the information, and then make good decisions. Critical thinkers don't look to someone else to tell them the answer. You are your own best source for answers.

Critical thinking is a powerful tool. Imagine figuring out how to start a fire, or connecting germs with disease, or inventing a telephone... or on a more practical level, how about just not wasting your money tomorrow? Critical thinking gives you the power to take control of your life.

Critical thinking sounds like something challenging or difficult. And just like everything else, a lot of people try to make critical thinking into something more complicated than it really is. Usually this is so they can benefit somehow. Most of the time money is involved.

And frequently it's just an insecure ego. Somehow,

making thinking seem more difficult makes them feel better about themselves for understanding it. Ironic when you realize a true critical thinker recognizes needless complications are just stupid.

We *Simplify*. You will find this concept prominent among our principles. We would rather encourage everyone to see how simple life can be. It takes stupid people to make it more complicated than it needs to be.

> By the way, "Simplify" is one of our principles of critical thinking. When we use a principle in our writing we put them in italics to identify them. We'll explain "Simplify" later in Principle #9.

The ability to think critically is being lost. People have developed great ability to look up answers. And it is truly amazing what you can find just by typing something into Google. Knowledge has never been easier to acquire.

But instead of using these powerful tools to gather knowledge, people just look up answers. Maybe that sounds efficient, but there's a problem. A quick search offers them many choices. Then instead of analyzing the question, people just choose an answer that sounds good. And what follows is a lot of stupidity. Bad answers get accepted, and then repeated over and over.

The herd mentality is taking over. Life in the mainstream has become comfortable enough that people just accept it and follow along.

At times there seems to be an unwritten agreement

between people who want to believe something, and any idiot willing to tell them a good story. The agreement is that neither of them will do any critical thinking. This is a dangerous and stupid way to go through life.

But some people stop to think about their world. They realize they're not as happy as they should be. They've done everything "right", but life isn't all that great.

You can see where it's all heading but you don't like that destination. Now what?

You start by stepping away from the herd. Getting out of the mainstream. You start using critical thinking to choose your own path.

There is an information overload today, along with an overload of bad answers. This is the first time in history humans have ever had to deal with this problem. In the millions of years of human evolution, it's only very recent history that's given us so much information to process.

And here's a fact, millions of years of evolution prove we don't need all that information. Somehow we got to over 7 billion humans on this planet without it. You need only a very small fraction of all the information that barrages you each day. Somehow humans got into at least the 1980's without 24-hour news, Huffington Post or Facebook. How did we ever survive?

You need a system to deal with all that data. You need a way to filter out all the bullshit. And you need a way to consider only the information that's truly important. You need critical thinking. Without it, you will stampede off the cliff along with the rest of the herd.

This book is going to invite you to think along with us. We are going to discuss our 11 basic principles, along with a few subtopics in some of them. Any one or more of them will help you make better decisions. If you eventually use all of them, and they become automatic in your life, you will become a critical thinking superstar. There is a reward for that; good decisions make your life a whole lot better.

There are only 11 principals used regularly, a couple more if you count the sub-parts. This is all you need to get the job done. Most questions do not require more than one or two principles applied before you get to your answer.

With practice, you get very efficient. Certain topics just naturally fit with certain principles. Many questions are actually the same question with just a different name. You can get very good at not wasting your time, which in turn allows you to answer more questions. More answers equal more power to choose your best course in life.

If you think about it, needing only 11 principles to address the vast majority of life's questions, that's pretty remarkable. Life really is pretty simple. We only go to eleven.

You're going to spend time thinking anyway. Why not make the best use of that time? Think critically. Make good decisions.

OK, let's get into it. Let's do some thinking together.

2.
What is Critical Thinking?

DEFINE THE TARGET. Critical Thinking – The objective analysis and evaluation of an issue in order to form a judgment.

The key part of that definition is **in order to form a judgment**. Critical Thinking comes BEFORE the judgment.

Do you notice how much more common it is to see people's judgments come first? People work very hard to believe what they want to believe. And that's stupid. It makes for some very entertaining stories though.

Nothing is more amusing than watching someone working hard to make their wrong answer be the right one. Remember when Ahmadinejad claimed there were no gay people in Iran? Still one of our favorites… not exactly a critical thinker there.

Or how about all the people who branded Galileo a heretic for proving the earth revolved around the sun. It is far easier to convince people they're at the center of the universe. I'll bet we could still convince a fair percentage of people Galileo was wrong, even today. But life is already difficult enough for stupid people.

You can argue all night that the sun isn't coming up in the morning, and it will still rise and prove you wrong.

It would have been much better to get a good night's sleep. Life is like that. You can think whatever you want and probably muddle through, but it's easier if you use the right answers.

A critical thinker has an easier life. They think about the questions before deciding on their answers. The right answer is a lot easier to accept when it finally shows up if you haven't already made a decision. The amount of energy stupid people waste trying to defend their wrong answers could be used to make their lives better. Instead, they waste it trying to make their wrong answer right.

Critical thinking is a method for dealing with the information overload we have today. You just let the data come in and apply critical thinking principles to determine its value. Most information is worthless and you will quickly reject it. It becomes automatic too. It wastes your time and that might even make you a little angry. Which is good because it helps you reject it faster next time.

Some information will be valuable. We need a little, a very small fraction of what is thrown at us every day, but we do need some. Gathering enough valuable information will take you to the answers you need. After you have what you need, the rest is rejected.

Once you know HOW to think, the rest is just plugging in the data. You pick the question, apply some critical thinking principles, and a short time later you have an answer that makes your life better.

The DontBeStupid.club Summary:

- Critical Thinking happens BEFORE a conclusion is reached.

- We have too much information. Critical thinking is how we find the little we need and reject the rest.

- Knowing HOW to think makes the rest easy.

3.
Principle 1: Open Mind

PRINCIPLE #1 IS the most important one to critical thinking. *Open Mind*. The right answer is of no use if you will not accept it. And you will think far more efficiently if you are not resisting the information as it comes in. Trying to make information fit some preconceived notion is far less efficient than just letting the information form the answer.

To be a good thinker, your beliefs have to be open to change. It's not scary. You won't change your mind every day. Most answers don't change. Once you have the right answer, it can last for a lifetime. And living with the wrong answer just wastes your time. Better to change your mind and be right as soon as possible.

This is Principle #1 because it all starts here. Many of our other principles can be considered in any order, but an Open Mind must always come first. With practice, it will become automatic. Positive reinforcement works. It really is more fun to be right than to be stubborn.

Critical thinking is applied in order to form a well-reasoned judgment. But you're just wasting your time if your brain cannot follow the path to the right answer. There is nothing to fear except maybe learning you've been wrong about something. And remaining wrong one second longer than necessary is really stupid. An open mind is our most valuable time saver.

An open mind may mean letting go of some cherished beliefs. Remember, as we mentioned before, Galileo was censured in his time for suggesting the earth revolved around the sun. He probably wasn't thrilled to figure that out and then find so many closed minds not wanting to hear it. But an open mind makes the right answer inescapable, even if you're the first one to see it. Poor Galileo. He was cursed with an open mind. But we can learn from him and other examples of great thinkers.

> "...and you will observe with concern how long a useful truth may be known and exist before it is generally received and practiced on."
>
> -B. Franklin.

Benjamin Franklin, the guy on the US $100 bill. He wrote that in 1786 about the dangers of ingesting lead. Wonder how many closed minds and children of closed minds were damaged before we started banning lead from water pipes about 200 years later. The estimates for replacing the lead water pipes still being used in the USA today range into hundreds of billions of dollars. Just stupid.

Another example? Louis Pasteur is credited with proving the germ theory of disease and disproving the theory of Spontaneous Generation. Prior to his proof, the world still believed living organisms sprouted from non-living matter. That was "science".

(By the way, use this as a cautionary tale. Naming

something a science doesn't prove anything. "Science" has been really stupid many times in history.)

Yes, today we all know that spontaneous generation is stupid. And Pasteur proved it elegantly in the middle 1800's. But you know what else? Other open-minded critical thinkers were saying the same thing back in the 1600's. That's 200 years earlier. How many people died unnecessarily until Pasteur came along? More often than we care to admit, the closed mind delays getting to the right answer with tragic consequences. That's stupid.

A doctor washing their hands was just silly in 1800. No one believed in things they could not see. That was proven wrong by the mid-1800's. And today? Compliance with hand cleansing is monitored at hospitals, and reports say progress is being made. Kind of amazing this useful truth needs enforcement to make it happen in hospitals... stupid.

Enormous energy is wasted trying to support opinions formed too early. Even more energy is wasted rejecting the right answers trying to hang on to mistaken beliefs. Life is easier with an open mind. You can watch people wear themselves out rationalizing their beliefs while you coast to the right answers because you did not make up your mind until after the facts were in.

Open Mind. It's the most important principle for critical thinking.

The DontBeStupid.club Summary:

- There's no point to critical thinking unless your mind is open to the answers.

- An open mind saves time and energy. It is difficult and costly to ignore the right answer or cling to false beliefs.

- Wash your hands.

4.
Principle 2: Define the Target

FIRST DEFINE WHAT you are thinking about. Then define the key terms you're using to think about it. A lot of stupidity is just confusion. Frequently, just taking the time to define the discussion is good enough to eliminate most of the clutter surrounding it and make the answer clear.

Just stop and ask "Exactly what answer are we after?" and "Are there any words where I'm not sure about the meaning?" If you're in a discussion with someone else, enlarge that second question to include "or where we don't agree on the meaning?"

Confusion is a fundamental problem with most opinions you hear. People don't answer the question, or they don't understand the word's used to describe it. Or they just think the question is a different one than you do.

A simple example might be saying to your mate "What's for dinner?" That can be either an invitation to discuss options or a request they serve you dinner. The ensuing conversation will be far more pleasant if both people understand the words the same way.

Very often, people change a question to suit their answer. We call this placing the target after the arrow has landed. Everyone hits the bulls-eye when you do it that way. But it's not critical thinking. You found no right answer. Reality won't move around to suit your shot. Adjusting the question to suit your answer just makes life more difficult.

For example, someone sleeps in and misses work. The original question they answered was "Do I want to get up or go back to sleep?". Then after they get fired, they decide they didn't want that job anyway. They just moved the target to suit their answer, but is life better or worse? Even if they really wanted to change jobs, there are much better ways to do it.

Changing the question is an annoyingly amateur debate technique too. If you've defined your target, it's easy to identify this tactic and avoid it. If a "moving target" happens in your discussions, just pause and say something like "that may be true but it's not what we were talking about". If you find yourself in too many of these discussions, don't waste your time. Change your discussion partner. And send the offender to chapter one to read about *Open Mind*. You're just talking with someone who wants to be right. Critical thinking would suggest you not waste your time.

Before any debate gets going too far, stop and ask yourself, "What is the target?". How will you know when the debate reaches its answer? For too many people, it ends when the other guy gives up. There is no specific answer being pursued, just the thrill of victory. You can avoid this pointless waste of energy by defining the target before you get too far into it.

If you find yourself disagreeing with your spouse about what to have for dinner, stop and *Define the Target*. Is it about health? Convenience? Money? How can you know what dinner to pursue until you have a common target?

Even if you're just thinking within yourself, you still must define your target. Critical thinking requires you to have a goal in the thought process. Letting your mind wander is OK too, it can be fun or relaxing, just don't expect to get any serious questions answered that way.

And you must always understand the words used in the discussion. It's not OK to continue thinking without understanding what has come before. You always have to know what path you're on. Whatever the subject, there will be terms that make it easier to understand.

A good test for this is to ask yourself "How would I explain this to someone else?". If an explanation doesn't quickly pop into your head, then you need to stop and define the terms for yourself. If you really understand it, then explaining it to someone else should be easy.

Don't let yourself off the hook too easily on this principle. People believe they know what they're doing far more than they really do. Most people's use of words is inexact. When someone understands key words in a discussion just a little differently, you end up in a debate that's really just semantics. And those are stupid.

The DontBeStupid.club Summary:

- Defining a discussion clearly is enough to find the answer in many cases.

- Critical thinking is goal-oriented. Without defining a goal, you have no path to follow.

- Define key terms used. Debate resulting from semantics is a waste of time.

- Don't waste time in discussions with people who try to use confusion to their advantage. They're not seeking the same goal as you.

5.
Principle 3: First Things First

IT IS TERRIBLY inefficient to put the cart in front of the horse. The tail does not wag the dog. You have to walk before you can run. The *First Things First* lesson has been taught before with many different metaphors.

There is an old Steve Martin joke that we will paraphrase here; "I know how to become a millionaire and not pay taxes. First get a million dollars. Then don't pay any tax on it. If the IRS knocks on your door, tell them you forgot."

That was funnier when Steve told it... but the joke was about violating the *First Things First* principle in a way so obvious it was funny. Skipping over the hard part is something people do way too often in their thought process.

But how often today do you see people more seriously adopting the same approach as Steve Martin? How many well-intentioned people have put in tremendous effort to get higher minimum wages laws while the number of "good" jobs in their district is declining? Smart? Or stupid? A critical thinker would consider putting that effort into creating higher paying jobs. Having a great minimum wage doesn't help much if no one is hiring.

How many debates will a government have over

financial programs with little to no impact on their budget deficits? The "safety net" programs in the US account for about 10% of the federal budget. Food stamps account for about 20% of that 10%, or 2% of the total budget. But you get raging debates going on in Congress over food stamps. *First Things First*. Fix Social Security/Medicare? That's about 40% of the total budget right there.

There is near mania over retirement planning today. And it's just stupid. Why would any critical thinker spend much time or resources for a payback that happens 30 or 40 years from now? It's stupid for anyone to assume they know what the priorities will be for all those years. (The same goal can be pursued without a 40-year commitment. Read our Investing book.)

There is no point to putting much effort into decisions when it's not clear if you will ever need them. This is especially true if there are more immediate challenges that need your energy first.

First Things First means you prioritize the decisions that have the most impact on your goal. You have only a finite amount of time to think of everything. If you use that time thinking about the trivial considerations, you never get to your goal. And if you get the big decisions right, the trivial ones tend to just follow along.

Facts having the biggest impact on your goal must be dealt with first. If your goal is to lose weight, it is stupid to stop putting cream in your coffee if you still drink two cokes a day. You have to look at your data and see what has the biggest impact on your goal. Chasing objectives that have little impact is a very inefficient use of energy.

Violating the *First Things First* principle can lead to good decisions that are useless because they have no impact on your goal. The "drop in an ocean" concept applies here. It does not help for you to conserve a glass of water while the power plant generating your electricity contaminates a million gallons.

Financial decisions require extra *First Things First* attention. So much advice given about money is just bad, people violate this principle all the time. For example, it is stupid to track your expenses in detail when only the biggest ones have a meaningful impact on your budget. That's a terrible waste of precious decision-making time and energy. It is stupid to save money by not going to Starbucks if you can't pay the mortgage.

Violating *First Things First* also leads to people giving up because their efforts seem to be wasted. And that is a terrible shame. For the same amount of effort, they could have gotten much more benefit. Life could be so much better if only their priorities were in the proper order.

It's really stupid to see how much mortgage you qualify for before even knowing if you should buy a house. Have you analyzed the rent vs. buy decision critically? After that, you want to know what's within your critically-thought-out budget, not what you "qualify for" using someone else's conditions (more on this in our Money book).

Some say eating dessert first is not following *First*

Things First, but that one doesn't stand up under critical thinking. *Open Mind*. If you're going to eat the whole meal anyway, you might as well eat it in whatever order you enjoy the most. Of course, if you still need the incentive to eat your veggies, then eating dessert last might still be a good idea.

First Things First is about being efficient. You will not necessarily make bad decisions if you ignore this principle, but the decisions you make will not have as much impact on your life as more important decisions where you make the same effort. You spend a finite amount of energy thinking, you have to make the most of it.

The DontBeStupid.club Summary:

- Putting the cart before the horse has never worked very well.

- The decisions with the biggest impact require the most attention.

- Don't waste time or energy making good decisions that have no impact.

6.
Principle 4: Common Sense

MOST OF YOUR life is lived on auto-pilot. Your body and your brain have been conditioned to make the right decisions to keep you alive. When something seems right (or wrong) before you think too much about it, in most cases you will be correct. It's your common sense.

Very frequently, a question is answered by nothing more than first *Defining the Target* and then applying *Common Sense*. It's amazing how many mistakes are made by people failing to define their target and then not giving their common sense a chance to work. We go too fast. Too much information. All those decisions we think we must make, everything we must get done today, it all creates a sense of urgency. And then we make mistakes because we move too fast to let common sense have any chance to help.

In our big rush to get everything done, we fail to use the thinking tool most readily at our disposal. You feel like you're going fast, but the problem is mistakes make life very inefficient. You go fast, expend a lot of energy, but don't get the best results. It is far better to slow down and make good decisions. If you make good decisions, you have fewer problems to think about later.

Common sense can be wrong. It's not always best to

stop your critical thinking process right after applying *Common Sense*. You just need to give it a chance to work. Common Sense is an opinion that has a place in any critical thinking process.

In the best case scenario, common sense agrees with a conclusion reached by more exacting data. And if your data leads you to a different answer, common sense just asks you to pause and be sure. Anytime you disagree with your common sense, you want to take a moment and be sure of your thought process.

A good exercise is to ask yourself why common sense disagrees with your answer. For example, I hate flying. Humans are not birds. We are not native to the sky. And we don't like confinement either. Common sense screams at me to stay out of airplanes. Using data, I can reach a critical thinking conclusion that flying is reasonably safe and my best choice if I need to travel 2,000 miles in one day. In this case, I will choose to overrule my common sense based on critical thinking. But common sense is not wrong, just overruled.

Most of the time when you see stupid behavior, it's because someone went too fast. Everyone has common sense; they just don't use it. Ironically, you can save a lot of time using common sense. Listening to it avoids a lot of stupid mistakes.

The DontBeStupid.club Summary:

- Most of your choices in life are made by common sense.

- You must give common sense the chance to work.

- Overrule common sense only when the alternative is critically thought out.

7.
Principle 5: Respect Nature

NATURE FUNCTIONS WITHOUT our input. The universe is vast, far more powerful than humans, and unaware of our existence. And nature is violent. Pushing too hard against nature usually doesn't work out very well for whoever is doing the pushing.

We need nature. Nature does not need us. Galileo may have proved the earth revolves around the sun, but centuries later humans still seem to believe they are at the center of the universe. A little critical thinking is all that's needed to get our heads straight about that idea.

We might impact the climate here on earth a little. We cause a little pollution, unleash a few deadly diseases, maybe melt a little ice, etc. But in the greater scheme of things Nature doesn't move for us at all. The logical conclusion of humans wrecking their habitat is the earth gets rid of humans. Kind of like when you get a fever to fight off an infection. Our body temp just goes up about 5 degrees while it fights off the disease. Might help to think about global warming that way. Another five degrees and you can say goodbye to Florida.

There are small battles against nature we can win. We certainly live longer now than people did 5,000 years ago. We've learned to prevent certain diseases. We've learned exercise can slow the effects of aging. And we manage gravity a little better, we can fly a little and build tall buildings that don't fall down.

But the power of nature is inevitable. The opposing force is just too big and unrelenting. Critical thinking demands we respect it in any decision where it has impact.

We don't intend *Respect Nature* to sound all fuzzy or ethereal. We're not "tree-huggers". We've driven through Utah and Nevada. Believe me, there is plenty of desolate landscape out there, perfect for landfills. Critical thinking makes it easy to see that garbage has a place to go for many more centuries.

But a force as big as nature must be included in any critical thinking process. Nature is going to have its impact whether we choose to respect it or not. Gravity is always going to pull everything toward the center of the earth, and it's much easier to paddle your boat in the direction the river is flowing.

Remember our example about flying back in the Common Sense chapter? I said I'd overrule my common sense and board a plane to get across country quickly. Plane travel is very safe today and it's a good choice for traveling 2,000 miles. But planes burn tremendous amounts of energy to stay in the air for relatively short periods of time. Anytime you avoid flying, it's never really a stupid decision it's just *Respecting Nature*. Gravity wants you on the ground.

Respect Nature does not mean we always go along with it. But it helps guide our critical thinking. Food and medicines are two great areas where we can apply this concept. Is it really such a good idea to use pesticides? Maybe drugs that interfere with the body's processes are misguided?

Respect Nature is also useful when considering human nature; how someone will react in any given circumstance. If you're going to diet, it helps to respect your nature. You're not going to eat food you hate. If you love blondes, don't marry a brunette.

And don't be shocked when you see humans killing each other, or think you can count on people to be peaceful. If you're a critical thinker, you already know the natural state of humans is trying to dominate each other. We like Captain Kirk's guidance here. "We can admit that we're killers, but we're not going to kill today. That's all it takes."

The killing acknowledgment is a bit harsh, but nature is not always pretty. An awful lot of stupid foreign policy happens because people don't want to admit human nature is what it is.

In any critical thought process, we can go against nature for a short time or in short doses. But for long-term strategy, it is better to respect nature. We may eat some candy and drink too much on holidays, but we will choose to feed our body what it really needs most of the time.

The DontBeStupid.club Summary:

- Nature is a force too big to ignore.

- We can run contrary to nature in short bursts, but it's bad long-term strategy.

- Choose not to kill today.

8.
Principle 6: Follow the Money

YOU'VE HEARD *Follow the Money* before as a concept, probably in a humorous anecdote. But do you routinely apply it in your thinking?

Money motivates most people's interaction with you. Most of the uninvited data you take in every day is intended to get money from you. Most of the decisions you find yourself considering will somehow involve spending money. Critical thinking requires following the money in most decisions.

Whenever you are in a buying situation, you must look for the money motive. Finding the profit and who gets it answers a lot of questions about whatever information you are considering. *Follow the Money*. Understanding the motives of the information providers helps you make good decisions.

You also have to be alert for situations that are not obvious buying situations. Going shopping at the store is obvious, but a lot of other situations are also about you buying something.

For example, assume you are sick. Your doctor gives you a prescription that cures your problem 75% of the time. Do you like your odds?

You cannot really know until you find out where the

75% data comes from. Who funded the study? Was it double blind? Was the sample size statistically significant? *Follow the Money*. Most drug studies are funded by the companies that want to sell their drugs. That has some impact on how much we trust the data and the drug. For example, many drugs prescribed score only a few points higher than a placebo. In those cases, we're willing to bet the money caused the results and not the drug.

Another example; there is a proliferation of "free" games you can download and play today. Once hooked on the game, you are offered many extras you can buy.

Facebook is "free". But they took in over $27 billion in revenue last year because they could promise advertisers you would see their programming.

Other examples include: you get offers for "free" interest on credit card transfers, but they're accompanied by transfer fees and high rates at the end of the free period. Buy-one-get-one-free is always a popular sales tactic. Always *Follow the Money*. Especially when you see something presented as "free".

In the world of financial products, you really have to *Follow the Money* to avoid mistakes.

For example, life insurance is a place where you really need to *Follow the Money*. When the agent says you need 10 times your annual salary in a Whole Life policy, *Follow the Money*. The salesman's commission on that policy ranges anywhere from 50% to 100% of the first year's premium. Do you really think he's motivated by your best interests? (If you need life insurance, buy a term life policy online. Just pick a highly rated company.)

You will see all kinds of pressure to save for retirement. *Follow the Money.* Who really benefits the most? Most of their motivation for selling you retirement investments is about what's best for their paycheck, not your retirement.

Money is a powerful motivator. It's the most common motivation for most interactions we deal with every day. And it causes many people to act in ways contrary to your best interests. Critical thinking demands we *Follow the Money* in all of those decisions.

The DontBeStupid.club Summary:

- Money is behind most of the data you think about each day, even in situations where your primary motive is not to buy something.

- When offered data, consider who funded the study that produced it.

- Nothing is really free.

- Consider the seller's profit motive whenever someone is telling you to buy something.

9.
Principle 7: Don't Be Distracted

CONFUSION DISTRACTS YOU, it takes you off your mission and makes it harder to get to the right answer. You have to stay on point. *Don't Be Distracted.*

Distraction is one of the most practiced skills in the world. Most of the messages trying to get you to do something are using distractions of some kind to dull your critical thinking process. Advertising is the most obvious offender.

For example, we all know sex sells. Should it? If you're buying porn, then yes, sex should sell it. But if you're buying a car? It's just a distraction. That car isn't going any faster, the beer isn't tasting any better, and your teeth aren't any whiter. You just got distracted.

We don't want to waste the words or space to talk about all the advertising distractions out there, they should be obvious to anyone remotely interested in critical thinking. Rihanna does not make Pepsi taste any better, but Pepsi sure does look better when Rihanna is drinking it.

Favorite Gallagher joke of all time; "Mr. Coffee hired Joe DiMaggio to say theirs was the best he ever tasted. This is quite an accolade for a cup of coffee."

Ignoring advertising is relatively easy. But there are

many more ways distraction is used to keep you from finding the right answers. These other methods are the bigger challenge for the critical thinker.

Names are used to cause confusion or misdirect to a different line of thought. For example, investing in a 401K is called "saving" for retirement. Saving is really something else. Investing in your 401K means betting that stocks and bonds will improve in value while you own them. The name change to "saving" just makes it sound better.

Name calling is used attempting to attach negative emotion to an idea. Watch how often someone insults someone else when they don't like what they're saying. *Don't Be Distracted* by insults.

The more people want to think about something, the more names it gets from people who want to appear smarter about it or help "guide" your thinking. Distinctions that make no difference must be ignored. This is a frequent *Don't Be Distracted* trigger. For most discussions, it really doesn't matter which of the 900,000 species of insects you're talking about. We just don't want bugs in our house.

Names are used to elicit a desired reaction. "Orange Roughy" is Slimehead. "Dried plums" are prunes. "Aggressive" investing is just taking greater risks. And the "Patriot Act" is among the least patriotic pieces of legislation you'll ever find.

Sorry about that last one. A political reference is so easy it's almost cheating. No one uses names trying to confuse us more than politicians, and no one else is so transparently stupid about it. Remember the Defense of

Marriage Act? *Don't Be Distracted*. Know the facts affecting your questions, not the names.

Telling you what you want to hear is a standard distraction technique. Beware of any compliment you receive from someone trying to sell you something. Enjoy it if you like, but it has no place in a critical thinking process. Men are surprisingly clever, and handsome too, when the saleswoman helps them buy presents for their wife.

Emotions are a bigger distraction. Compliments are easy to spot and ignore. But emotional manipulations are more difficult. Most of us can control our ego if we must, but emotions are much tougher. You really deserve the retirement of your dreams, you worked hard for so long, you've earned it! Of course you "feel" that way. And then you start buying whatever they're selling...

Another standard distraction technique is to state facts no one can disagree with, and then attach something else to the sequence. For example; It would be terrible if your children die from mosquito bites, you need to use our repellent.

A variation on this technique of stating facts first is the "after this, therefore because of this" approach. It's terribly flawed logic, but people get away with it all the time. Once you get accustomed to spotting this distraction, you will automatically exclude it from your decision-making process.

An example to make the point; "I had chicken for dinner last night and it's raining this morning, therefore my chicken dinner caused this rain."

That was ridiculous to make it clear. Now try this one; "The NSA has been reading your emails for the last two years. We've had no terrorists bomb American buildings for the last two years. Therefore, the NSA surveillance worked."

Don't Be Distracted. To a critical thinker, NSA surveillance sounds just like the chicken dinner.

Always watch for the subtle variations on this cause and effect theme. Politicians are the biggest abusers, but everyone trying to persuade you they have the "right" answer will get around to trying it sooner or later. Any good thing that happens, you can bet someone will try to claim something they did was the cause.

Entertainment is frequently used as a distraction to advance a point of view. One of the stupidest things we've started doing is treat entertainment as a knowledge source. "Inspired by real events" is becoming the same thing as a documentary in the minds of the viewers.

Define the Target. Entertainment – Providing amusement or enjoyment. Entertainment is not about facts, and it's not about critical thinking, that's for sure. Anyone who thinks the size of an audience correlates with expertise... well, that's stupid.

Don't Be Distracted. Movies are not history. Comedy shows are not news, and neither are the "serious" news commentary shows either. Most "news" today is just entertainment with a few facts sprinkled in to grab the most audience. Do you ever notice all the great legs on Fox News? Much appreciated. But we don't make decisions based on them. *Don't Be Distracted.*

The DontBeStupid.club Summary:

- Confusion is used to keep you stupid.

- Names are used to take you off the critical thinking path.

- Sex is a huge distraction.

- Entertainment is a distraction. Not a source of facts.

- Joe DiMaggio was married to Marilyn Monroe.

10.
Principle 8: There Will Be Math

NO MATTER WHAT you're thinking about, a little data helps. Understanding some math helps you understand what the data means. More often than not, what you hear around you is bad math. It's being used to convince you of something stupid.

There Will Be Math is one of the larger, most challenging, categories in our principles. But the world is a mathematical place. Math was developed by humans as part of our language to explain the world. Math is a universal language. You have to speak it well enough to make good decisions.

Now don't worry, this isn't a math book and we're not talking about calculus here. But you need to do enough math to draw conclusions from your data. You need to understand enough math to know who is being stupid and who is trying to manipulate your thinking. Fortunately, this rarely requires going beyond add, subtract, multiply and divide.

Most of the time *There Will Be Math* is not challenging, you just need to take the time and actually do the addition or subtraction. You really can't decide to buy a home without doing a rent versus buy analysis. Just take the time to total up two columns and compare.

To make a good decision between job opportunities,

you have to add up what the fringe benefits are worth. And also add in commuting costs. To make your best choice, you have to do some additions and subtractions and not just look at the salary they are offering.

There Will Be Math means you have to venture into statistics a little too. But you don't have to be a statistician, you just need to understand how they're used to manipulate your thinking. It is not an exaggeration to say that most of the times statistics are used trying to convince you of something, those statistics being used are meaningless.

If you have an honest coin and flip heads four times in a row, it's nothing special. It will happen more than 6% of the times you flip a coin four times. Something that happens 6% of the time is not rare. You would not make a major decision based on that limited number or trials. But this approach of a statistically insignificant number of trials is used to justify selling you countless items.

An everyday example for people on prescription meds goes like this: Out of 100 people taking this drug, only 2 died. Among 100 people not taking the drug, 3 died. This drug reduces chances of death by 50%. That kind of bad math is used to sell billions of dollars' worth of drugs.

Bad statistics are everywhere when it comes to trying to convince people of something stupid.

ROI, return on investment, is some math you need to do regularly. Obviously it's important when you decide what to do with your money. But you also need to apply it to the rest of your life. We have a finite amount of time and an infinite number of things we can do with it. In order to set priorities, we need to figure out what offers the best return on your invested time. For example, if your house is already pretty clean, then vacuuming again today has limited value. Maybe there's more ROI for that time spent elsewhere?

There Will Be Math also means you have to understand scaling. *Define the Target* - Scaling. A progression or graduated series. Scaling numbers is a tactic frequently used to convince you of something. Like when they show you a curve of how much money you'll have 40 years from now if you just start giving them some of your money today.

Recently, the most common use of scaling seems to be health organizations trying to whip up a frenzy over whatever the latest disease. If you're over 40, you probably remember the whole world should have AIDS by now. I think bird flu is supposed to have wiped us out by now too. We're fond of showing a financial example using sales materials from other people where if we just add a few more years to their scale, you have all the money in the world. *There Will Be Math*. Critical thinkers can see when scaling is being used to manipulate their thinking.

At some point large numbers get so large they're just "big". It's difficult to comprehend the difference between a billion and a trillion. They're just BIG. But that is not specific enough to make good decisions. For example, *There Will Be Math*. Can you figure out how the USA will ever pay off the national debt? Or what is likely to happen with Social Security by the time you want to claim it? These answers might affect how you vote. Critical thinkers do the math.

The concept of diminishing returns is important in *There Will Be Math* too. You have to identify when further effort is yielding less results. Data becomes less meaningful the more of it you get. Money buys less important stuff the more you get. Disciplining your kids is less effective the more you do it. Meetings are less productive the more you attend. Whenever a quantity of anything is involved, you have to identify when you have enough, and when more will not be worth the effort.

And our final point on *There Will Be Math*. People lie, numbers do not. Math is your friend, and it stops stupidity even faster than nature.

The DontBeStupid.club Summary:

- Math is all around us, it's a universal language.

- Math is needed to evaluate data.

- Statistics are usually distorted in any sales situation.

- Numbers don't lie. Math is a powerful weapon against stupidity.

11.
Principle 9: Simplify

OUR *SIMPLIFY* PRINCIPLE was inspired by C.W. Ceram;

> *"Genius is the ability to reduce the complicated to the simple."*

If there is one principle on which we would like to be judged, this is the one. We do not consider ourselves smart about any topic unless we can *Simplify* it.

Life is simple. Some things are a little more complicated than others, but nothing is really too complicated. You drop an apple and it falls to the ground. Gravity doesn't get complicated until you try to make the answer different. Then to make life more difficult, you can try to convince someone else your different answer is right. And then maybe you get them to jump off a building trying to fly.

People work very hard to make things more complex. If they get to write the rules, then of course they give themselves an advantage over anyone else getting into the game later. *Respect Nature*. This is instinctive behavior. Humans have always tried to gain advantage over other humans. It takes critical thinking to break out of this cycle.

At DontBeStupid.club we *Simplify*. Whatever topic is being discussed, we know it can be made simple enough for everyone to understand.

Complications are only added to advance someone's agenda. Someone is trying to impress you with how smart they are, or how much more money they're worth. Making money and satisfying an insecure ego probably account for 90% of human motivation. It is most efficient to look for one or both of these as the first step in trying to simplify anything.

Many "professional" service providers rely on added complications to validate their fees and salaries. Frequently they have certificates or even licenses demonstrating their considerable understanding of these complications. More often than not, you're better off without them.

And if the people adding complications happen to be in a position of power, then the complications are usually attempts to control you.

Here's our favorite example. The first ten amendments to the US constitution are commonly referred to as the "Bill of Rights". They contain less than 500 words total. All ten amendments, less than 500 words total. Freedom of speech, the right bear arms, etc., all handled in less than 500 words. James Madison was a genius, by Ceram's definition or anyone else's.

The US "Patriot Act" has over 50,000 words in it. "Obamacare" has over 300,000 words. We'll leave you to draw your own conclusions about those authors.

We think everyone has heard of the KISS concept. Keep It Simple Stupid. Just for fun, we want to elaborate a little because most people don't have it right. "Keep It Simple" is clear enough, but the "Stupid" part is not calling the listener stupid. The "Stupid" in KISS is a reference to making the product or explanation so simple that even a stupid person can understand it. It could be more clearly stated as "Keep It Stupidly Simple". We like this original meaning better. It offers the clearest statement of the intentions behind our *Simplify* principle.

Occam's Razor is another good simplifying message, also somewhat distorted in the public's understanding. (notice a pattern here? Stupid people have been distorting these answers...)

The Razor states that when confronted with multiple hypotheses to solve a previously unsolved problem, the simplest explanation should be selected first. This is a good message for critical thinkers addressing a new problem. The Razor is NOT the simplest answer is usually right. And only stupid people go through life thinking the easiest answers are usually correct.

The need to *Simplify* is everywhere. When warning labels get too long, no one reads them. When there are too many laws, people ignore them. When there is too much data, people just accept stupid answers. The failure to *Simplify* yields the opposite of the desired result.

In our Investing book, we simplify over 7,000 mutual fund choices into just a few that are worth looking at. We use a combination of *There Will Be Math* and *Simplify*. But 7,000 choices? No wonder people think investing is difficult. *Follow the Money*. Who benefits as a result of those complications? Not you, that's for sure.

Whatever goal is being pursued, it is easier to get

there when it is made simple.

The DontBeStupid.club Summary:

- True genius keeps things simple.

- Complications are added by people trying to gain some advantage.

- As usual, politicians today are among the worst offenders.

- Your goals are easier to attain when you keep things simple.

12.
Principle 10: Learn from History

WE HAVE ALL been here before. With thanks to CSNY, we're borrowing Déjà Vu for our principle. *Learn from History*. Very often you can see the future by looking into the past.

Names change, but people stay the same. Many of the problems you think about today are just repeats of something that has happened before. And it would be stupid not to learn from those experiences. Some very smart people have already thought about many things for us.

Are you shocked at corruption in positions of power? Why? History has shown us that giving people power is the surest way to corrupt them. Governments, churches, soccer leagues, it doesn't matter. If you allow people too much power, they become corrupt. The most famous quote on the subject is by Lord Acton back in 1887.

> *"Power tends to corrupt, and absolute power corrupts absolutely. Great men are almost always bad men."*

Learn from History. If you give people too much power they will become corrupt.

It's why the founding fathers of the USA put three

branches of government in place. They are supposed to hold each other in check. "Gridlock" is part of the design. I imagine they would have made 10 branches if they could have foreseen all the power madness that has come in over the years.

Are government deficits and high taxes a surprise? *Learn from History*. Virtually every major world power that has come before in history has collapsed under financial strain. Given the opportunity, governments will always spend more money than they have. Wouldn't it be more efficient to include this knowledge in the decision-making process? Whenever the idea of a Balanced Budget Amendment comes up, it's amazing how people refuse to *Learn from History* while debating it. Even without taking any position on the topic, a critical thinker can at least frame a more productive debate.

Will deficit spending affect your money? Don't be stupid, of course it will. *Learn from History*. Every national currency has failed at some point due to the government acting stupidly. Putting too much faith in Dollars or Euros or whatever the dominant currency at this time would be stupid. All you have to do is *Learn from History*. Every government running deficits for too long finally collapsed along with their "money". Nothing new is going on now.

A critical thinker will not let their government limit the definition of "money" to only their currency. A critical thinker can use history as a guide to find better answers. If you look, you can learn from multiple examples of protected wealth in countries where the currency has gone bust. Usually it involves some variation on holding physical assets like land instead of currency. (Governments define currency. Physical assets define themselves. Read our Money and Investing books for more.)

The entire history of the human race is built on conquering and subjugating the people around them. Parts of the world are more civilized today and conduct their wars with money. And parts are still conducting wars with killing as usual, subjugating their neighbors with weapons. Either way, history shows us that humans are always going to be seeking an advantage over one another. *Learn from History*. Maybe foreign policy plans that presume different behavior are stupid?

How about economic inequality? *Learn from History*. There has always been "the 1%". When you read history, do you assume everyone was a baron living in a castle? Of course not. The vast majority of people in every civilization have always been poor. There is always this tendency to identify with those who were in the top 1%. But 99% of people lived and died underneath them. Today is no different. If you want to think critically about this issue, read "The Gospel of Wealth" on our website. *Learn from History*. Andrew Carnegie understood capitalism.

Sometimes you can learn from your own history. If something worked before, of course you'd do it again. And if you've made a mistake before, it's very efficient to be sure you don't repeat it. If your last diet failed, it's probably a waste of time to choose that same diet again.

In any critical thinking process, it's efficient to pause and see if some other smart person has dealt with the same question. And some of those people were incredibly smart. It would be stupid not to learn from the experiences of history.

The DontBeStupid.club Summary:

- Nothing much new really happens. We have all been here before.

- Throughout history, great civilizations and great individual minds have dealt with the same questions.

- It's efficient to learn from the experiences of other great thinkers.

13.
Principle 11: Think for Yourself

YOUR LIFE IS all planned out for you before you have a chance to make any choices. We have an illusion of freedom. We may choose a school or a job, but the path is the same one as everyone else's. You have a student loan, a mortgage, a car loan, maybe some kids... The whole herd is headed in the same direction.

If you don't like where you're heading, just step out of the mainstream. *Think for Yourself.* Prove you are really free by deciding to choose your own path. Right now, think of something everyone does that is stupid. Now stop doing it. If you need a place to start, stop borrowing money. It's stupid. And everyone does it. If that's too hard, stop drinking soda. It's stupid. Per capita consumption in the US is about 44 gallons annually. Or cook at home one more day per week. Whatever you do, choose something smart and prove you have a free will.

And you know what? The first time is the hardest. Once you start down the path, the next choices get easier and easier. None of us really wants to be stupid. The world did it to us before we had the chance to think critically. *Think for Yourself* is the most rewarding of our principles. You feel great when you use your free will.

Remember the story Emperor's New Clothes? Please

feel free to visit our website where you can read the entire story. The Emperor's New Clothes is a cautionary tale written about people's failure to think for themselves. Everyone is too afraid of thinking differently from the person next to them.

An awful lot of stupid behavior is just the herd mentality, driven by those who benefit from it. You know, slaughterhouses are designed based on the animals following the one ahead of them. A whole herd will run right off the side of a cliff just following along.

Humans get to choose. You don't really have to follow along. Humans are not really herd animals. It's not how we evolved. That behavior is conditioned into us by those who benefit. And it gets more dangerous all the time. You must use critical thinking and step away from the herd to make your life better.

Do you really think it's OK that 60% of Americans are taking at least one prescription drug? Does that sound smart, or stupid? But if your cholesterol is 240 and you say "no" to the statins, at minimum you will have to endure the scorn of the masses. But they're wrong. *Think for Yourself.* Step away from the herd.

Do you think it's OK for the herd to have trillions of dollars in debt to pay off? Refuse to borrow and see how many people call you crazy. *Think for Yourself.* Step away from the herd.

The above examples are places where critical thinking will tell you to step away from the herd. We chose them deliberately because they impact so many people. Critical thinking will get you to those answers. But you have to *Think for Yourself* if you want to act on them. Do not let the herd think for you.

Our goal is always to be like the child in the Emperor's New Clothes. See everything through your own eyes, *Think for Yourself* and don't just see what everyone else tells you is there.

The DontBeStupid.club Summary:

- Humans are not evolved as herd animals. You can *Think for Yourself*.

- The herd mentality is driven by those who benefit from our stupid choices.

- See everything for yourself. Do not see anything just because someone else says so.

14.
Putting It All Together

LET'S DO A real life critical thinking example for a relatively common decision that has a serious impact on someone's quality of life.

I get into my normally reliable, paid-off debt-free car to go to work this morning, back out of the driveway, stop and shift into "Drive". As I accelerate forward, I notice the engine seems to be getting louder. As I reach 20 MPH I notice the car is not shifting gears. My transmission is stuck in first gear.

First Things First. Can I continue driving? My tachometer tells me the engine is OK up to 6000 RPM, and I'm cruising along right now at about 4500 RPM, so I should be able to continue driving without immediate concern. I'm just not able to keep up with traffic. I'll drive in the right lane with my flashers on and let people honk at me. My day is already worse than theirs, so honk away, I don't care.

I patiently drive slowly to my trusted mechanic. The diagnosis is my transmission needs a total rebuild. And I'm quoted a price of $2,500 for the job. Now what?

Well, this car is 9 years old. It's paid off and I have the title in my drawer at home, but it has 110,000 miles on it, a couple of minor dings in the paint and a rip in the rear seat upholstery. And honestly, I'm tired of this car.

It was three years old when I bought it, I've been driving it for 6 years, and it's a boring 4-door sedan model. But I've taken good care of it, I really do have a good mechanic, and he says the car is in good shape overall, just the transmission is dead.

But I'd really like a new car. I've seen ads with monthly payments at $399. The $2,500 I'd spend on this repair is plenty for a down-payment. In fact, I can probably get away with $1,000 down and save $1,500 cash right at the start. So for the same money I'd spend today repairing my old car, I think I can get a new car with enough cash left over to cover almost the first 4 payments. Let's go shopping!

Wait a minute. A critical thinker does not make emotional decisions when this kind of money is on the line. I need to evaluate this decision critically. Do I repair or buy new? Wait a minute again...

Keep an *Open Mind*. I should not needlessly limit my choices. There are more options than just the convenient "either or" choice here.

First Things First. Do I need a car at all? This answer could be "no" under some people's circumstances, and the critical thinking process would take a different path. For example, if you have great public transit available, then you may choose not to repair or replace. But for this example, I will say "Yes", I commute 15 miles to work and there is no public transit in my area, so I definitely need a car.

I need a car. This one must be fixed or replaced. *Think for Yourself*. I must not allow myself to be a victim of all that advertising. This is an expensive decision, I want to think critically and not be stupid. I must ignore the emotions telling me to buy a new car. *There Will Be Math*. I must estimate the cost of both choices to make my best decision.

The cost for repairing my car is pretty clear. My trusted mechanic has quoted $2,500 "out the door" for the rebuild. *Define the Target*. I confirmed "out the door" includes all taxes. Rebuild cost equals $2,500. Done.

For my new car, I've had my eye on a cool "crossover" SUV. I now quickly research it online and find that "all in" it will cost $36,000. The ad said $32,999 but that wasn't real. After I added in everything the ad did not include, the dealer quoted me $36,000 "all in". *Define the Target*. "All in" did not include sales tax. Sales tax is another $2,880. So my total purchase cost is now $38,880. With $1,000 down payment, my loan payment will be $690 per month. Whoa! That's not $399 like I was dreaming about... turns out the add assumed 10% down on that $32,999 price and that you'd also pay the sales tax in full at time of purchase.

I better pause for a moment and let *Common Sense* get a chance to work here. I'm going to pay $1,690 to get out the door with my new car, and $690 per month for 5 years? There is no way this is going to be a good financial decision compared to my $2,500 repair.

But my friends tell me to buy the new car, like they did. They say don't pay good money to repair an old car? *Think for Yourself*. This is a herd mentality with everyone thinking as they've been programmed. There is no new data here, just unsupported opinions.

Learn from History. About 9 times out of 10 people make

the stupid emotional decision when confronted with this repair or replace decision for their car. Billions in advertising has prepared them (badly) for the decision. Learning from their experiences can provide lessons I do not need to learn for myself. My friend has been "broke" for five years while covering the $600 monthly payment for his new SUV. Do I really want to suffer like that?

Then the dealer says "take it home for the night. If you don't want to keep it, just bring it back in the morning." Wow! (That really worked on me once, by the way. I paid cash so it was not an incredibly stupid decision, but no question the selling tactic had more influence than it should... nobody's perfect.) *Don't Be Distracted.* My *Common Sense* is not going to be overruled by an overnight test drive this time.

What if I give up on the idea of a cool new SUV, what now? *Simplify.* I can only consider choices that have much lower payments. The only way I can get my cool SUV is to look at a used model.

Now I find an SUV I like, it's 4 years old and has 40,000 miles on it, but I can get my payment all the way down to $299, and for only 48 months instead of 60. That costs me a total of $14,352 in payments plus my $1,000 down payment, or $15,352 total.

Wait a minute. I would have to pay to transfer my license plates. $600. That sounds like a lot! My plates only cost me $300 when I renewed them 6 months ago. Now I learn that license plates are based on the approximate car value in my state. A new car pays the highest rate. Older cars are cheapest. OK, I have to add in $300 per year of increased license cost.

Now I call my insurance agent. Wow! Insurance on the SUV is almost 50% more. Instead of $700 per year, now I'd be paying $1,000 per year for insurance. OK, I have to add in another $300 per year for insurance. My insurance agent recommends I buy the new car. He says his experience has shown that people are better off when they buy the new car instead of repair the old one. *Follow the Money*. He makes more money if I buy the new car. And he has not given me any new data to consider, just words. There is no value to this advice, I ignore it.

There Will Be Math. So at the end of the next 48 months, my newer SUV will have cost me $17,752 more than keeping my paid-off car. I just have to fix my car.

I can pay $2,500 and repair my boring old sedan today, plus budget for whatever additional repairs it might need over the next 4 years. My mechanic tells me my sedan is in good shape and should last at least another 5 years without major repair. I'll need brakes and tires plus routine maintenance, about $1,000. *Learn from History*. I'm going to add in another $500 because something unexpected always happens. So I will add a total of $1,500 to the cost of my transmission repair. That puts my total for "repair" at $4,000 for the same 48 months it would take to pay off the newer SUV.

First Things First. If financial consideration is my only concern, then I'm done. $17,752 is a lot more money than $4,000. I can do a lot of better things over the next four years with that $13,752 difference. Get on with the repair!

For most people, that should end the critical thinking process. Repairing the old car is a "no-brainer" to a critical thinker in this scenario. Only the emotions can sway you away from the right answer. *Don't Be Distracted*.

But let's try to make this more interesting. Here are two possible scenarios where I might want to continue with more critical thinking.

Let's say I've been wanting to start my own business on the side, and I need to haul some gear that won't fit in my sedan. And occasionally I will have to drive a customer in my car too, so I need the newer SUV to make a better impression. Now what?

There Will Be Math. If I expect to make $14,000 additional off this side business over the next 48 months, then it pays for the difference and I should buy the new car.

Or, let's say I've been career driven for too long and have neglected my love life. And my old sedan is just not going to send the right message to any potential dinner dates where I'm doing the driving. *Respect Nature*. Nothing is more powerful in humans than the urge to mate. Happiness in life is strongly correlated to having a strong primary relationship. I'd spend the extra $13,752 without hesitation and get on with the search for lifetime happiness.

Whatever my decision, I will have no doubts about it. I know it's right. I got to it using critical thinking. I did not act as a stupid herd animal programmed to do what someone else wants me to do.

DontBeStupid.club Summary:

- Critical thinking can guide you through potentially expensive situations where you've been programmed to make the wrong decision.

- Critical thinking will take you to the right answer. In this case, it could be either repair or replace depending on goals. And it could also have been "neither" if circumstances were different.

15.
Bonus Principle: Time is Priceless

TIME IS A finite resource. None of us has enough of it. All of us want more time. And critical thinking is a way to get more time in our life.

We don't have enough time in our life to waste any on stupidity. We'll waste time drinking wine, or watching the football game, or maybe even dancing. But wasting time being stupid, well that's just stupid.

You can cling to wrong beliefs. Or your *Open Mind* can allow the right answer to make your life easier.

You can waste time on decisions with no impact, or *First Things First* you can get priorities in order and make the decisions that improve your life the most.

You can row against the current, or you can *Respect Nature* and paddle your boat in the direction the river is flowing.

You can look at all the pretty pictures, or *Don't Be Distracted*, you can make decisions based only on the data that matters.

You can waste time on semantics, or you can *Define Your Target* and get to the point.

You can rush to make too many decisions, or you can give your *Common Sense* a chance to work.

You can waste hours each month trying to balance your budget and track your spending. Or *There Will Be Math*. You can do it right once and then use those hours you save each month to do something else.

You can *Follow the Money* and quickly decide if the information is valid.

You can *Simplify*, saving your time and making the decisions easier at the same time. Simplifying is very efficient.

You can *Learn from History* and make a decision in seconds because you agree with someone else who was very smart about it. Or you can spend time trying to reinvent the wheel.

You can step away from herd and *Think for Yourself*. Nothing is more personally rewarding.

How much time can you gain by applying our 11 principles? How much time can you add back into your life just by thinking critically? The answers build on each other and you never reach the end.

The less time we spend on a decision, the more decisions we can make. Or we can choose to waste some time on things more fun than problem-solving. Critical thinking gives you more time for life.

H. Granville James

The DontBeStupid.club Summary:

- Time is a finite resource, too valuable to waste on stupidity.

- Critical thinking lets us make more decisions in the time we have.

- More good decisions make our life better.

- There is no limit on the number of good decisions we can make.

58

16.
Final Thoughts

WELL THAT'S IT. Eleven critical thinking principles we live by. And we also value our time enormously.

We are overloaded with information today. Critical thinking helps us take control of that overload and turn it into something that can make our lives better.

Our critical thinking method is not difficult. You can start looking for the stupidity around you right away. The *Open Mind* comes first, *Define Your Target* next, and then *First Things First*. After that it really doesn't matter too much what order you use for the rest of the principles. They all help.

In our case, we probably use *There Will Be Math* and *Don't Be Distracted* the most. They just work for us. After a little practice, you will find whatever works for you. Some people like math, some people like history. There are usually several paths to the right answer.

We take *Think for Yourself* for granted now. We think following the herd is more dangerous than just about any other choice available right now. When we see the herd doing something, we are immediately suspicious. The rewards of *Think for Yourself* make it self-sustaining.

Critical thinking sounds harder than it is. And just like

everything else, a lot of people try to make it more complicated so they can benefit. Everyone is seeking an advantage in this relatively simple game of life. There's no reason to let them have one. Always remember to *Simplify*. There is absolutely nothing out there that cannot be reduced to simple terms. Even critical thinking.

In most of your encounters each day, stupidity is encouraged so people can get your money. But sometimes they just want to control you, or build up their own ego. Whatever the motives, the rest of the world tries very hard to make you think stupidly.

The more stupid we are, the more it costs us. Time, anxiety, cash, and frequently pain and suffering too. And Stupidity is BIG business. Everywhere we are stupid, someone else is collecting the cash.

Applying the DontBeStupid.club critical thinking principles can break this cycle. One topic at a time. We can all find the answers.

Hopefully we made a contribution here, and we are all better at critical thinking.

17.
Don't Be Stupid Club

AT DONTBESTUPID.CLUB WE make the world a little less stupid.

We think critically. We start with an *Open Mind*. Then we apply our principles and think about the question. A little critical thinking is all that's required to quickly reach most answers. Sometimes a little more work is required. But we always get to the answer.

We really don't care what people think. But we do care about how they think. Any well-reasoned opinion deserves respect. And opinions without basis are just stupid. Differing answers are fine. All we want is to make the world a little less stupid. If you hate our answer and have a well-reasoned opposition, GREAT!

We're all in this adventure together. We're stupid too. We are all conditioned from birth to think the wrong way. But hopefully we are a little less stupid for trying to fix that.

Critical thinking is a skill that can be learned. It's not even a difficult skill. It's harder to be a good welder or good coder or good baseball player. It's impossible for most of us to dunk a basketball. But we all can be good thinkers.

Critical thinking is a way of looking at the world. It's a

framework for thinking about anything. You're going to spend time thinking anyway, why not make the most of it? We think life is easier this way. You never feel lost if you know how to think.

Most disagreements we observe just come from people violating our principles. Arguing points without defining their targets... adding complexity to hide their own inadequacies... trying to bullshit their way to a profit... going against nature... doing the wrong things first... all just stupid.

The world can be a much better place if we are all a little less stupid.

And know this. If you are one of us, then you are never stupid. The stupidity is all around you, but it can never get YOU! Critical thinking is stronger than stupidity. Answers always equal power.

Our goal is to make a little difference in your life and entertain. Let us know how we did. We'd love to hear from you.

Visit http://DontBeStupid.club if you'd like more.

Our Amazon Store is located at: http://astore.amazon.com/dontbclub-20. It's where you'll find some of the products we like. Nothing in our store is stupid. You don't pay anything extra, but we get a little commission if you buy here. And we appreciate it. It helps us keep making the world a little less stupid.

We thank you for the time you spent with us.

Made in the USA
Las Vegas, NV
30 August 2022

54354702R00039